HOW TO DRAW
WILD ANIMALS

Jennifer Bell

Award Publications Limited

ISBN 978-1-84135-988-5

Published by Award Publications Limited, The Old Riding School, The Welbeck Estate, Worksop, S80 3LR

15 1 Printed in China

Drawing wild animals is easy if you...

...find an easy way to do it!

So start SIMPLE

Even the most complicated drawing is made up of simple shapes.

circles

smaller

small

tiny

big

bigger

Egg shapes are useful!

ovals

Practise drawing overlapping circles and ovals – they don't have to be perfect!

Overlap shapes to build bigger shapes!

Heads and necks

long neck

short neck

wedge

oval

triangle

And stick legs!

long legs

short legs

Lines with little circles for joints (where the legs bend) and for paws.

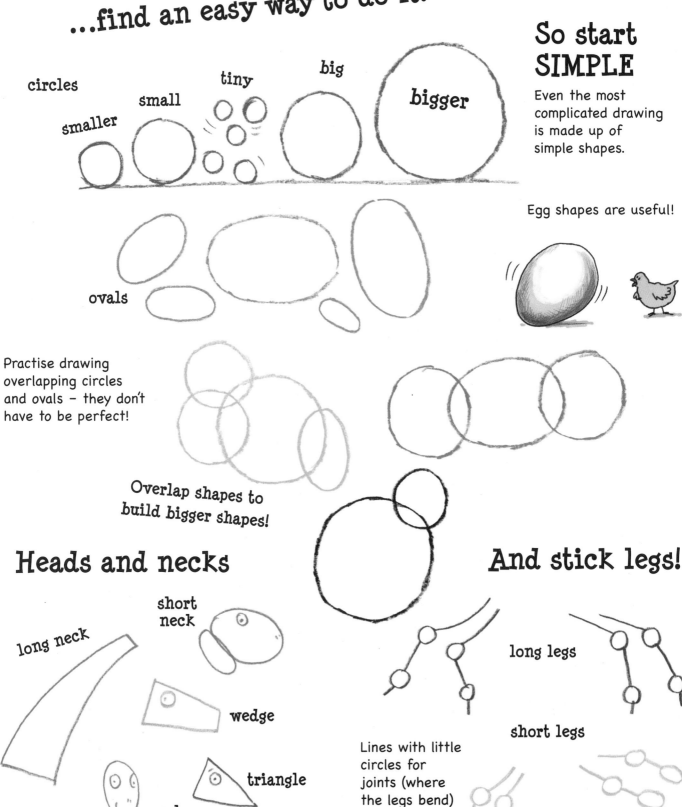

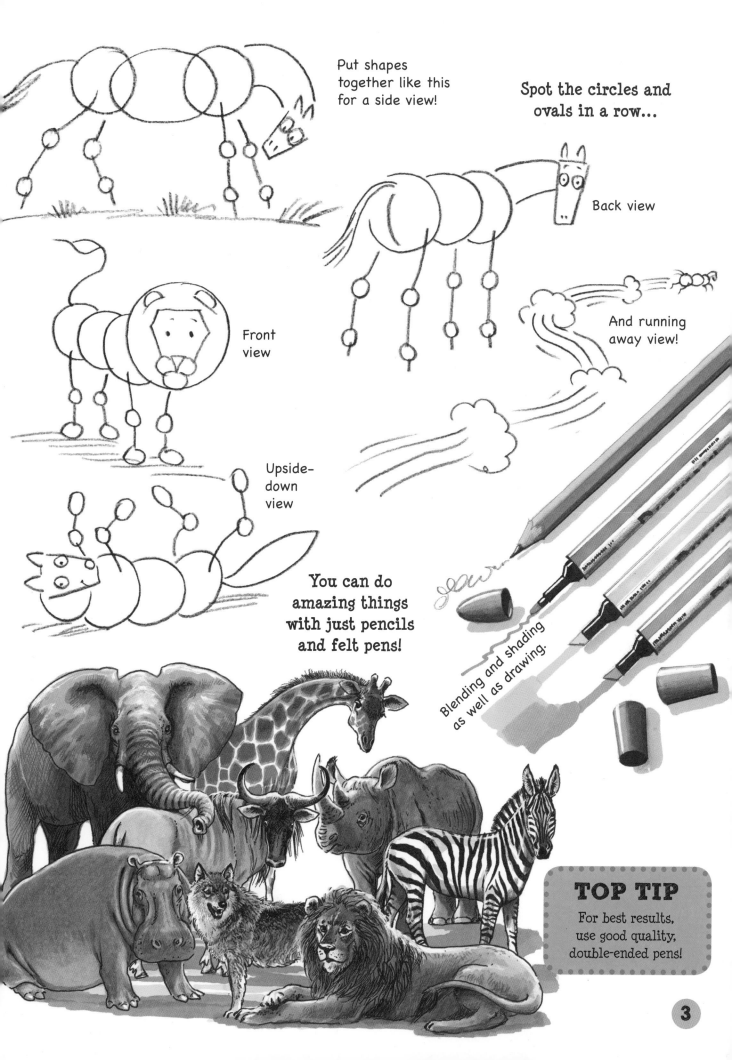

Put shapes together like this for a side view!

Spot the circles and ovals in a row...

Back view

Front view

And running away view!

Upside-down view

You can do amazing things with just pencils and felt pens!

Blending and shading as well as drawing.

TOP TIP
For best results, use good quality, double-ended pens!

Hippo

Step 1 ▼ An easy start! Draw an oval for the body, with two circles inside it for haunches.

Step 2 ▶ Add a circle and another smaller overlapping circle for a head and a snout. Draw lines and circles for legs, knees and feet.

Step 3 ▶ Draw an outline around the body, legs and feet. Add ears, eyes, nostrils and a mouth.

Step 4 ▶ Add pencil lines to show shadows and texture on the skin.

Hippo-water-mus!

4

Hippo in the water

Step 1 ▼ First draw a line for the water. Above it, draw a large curved line for the hippo's back. Add a circle for a head.

Step 2 ▼ Add a curved line for a neck, one circle for an eye and two circles for a mouth. Draw three curved lines joining the circles together, like this.

Step 3 ▼ Draw sharp, pointy teeth along the bottom jaw and short, stubby teeth along the top. Add an ear, eye, nostril and some neck wrinkles, too.

Step 4 ▼ Add an outline around the body and rub out your pencil marks. Colour with thick, pink strokes. Blend in a layer of medium grey. Leave some pink bits showing too!

Mud, mud, glorious mud!

Some of the hippo's teeth are as long as 40 cm!

You're beautiful, Mum!

To make your picture more realistic, add some shadows to the water, and some tiny drops of white paint to make it sparkle!

Lion

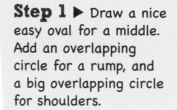

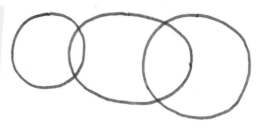

Step 1 ▶ Draw a nice easy oval for a middle. Add an overlapping circle for a rump, and a big overlapping circle for shoulders.

Step 2 ▶ Add another big circle for a head and mane. Draw lines and circles for legs, knees and paws. Add lines for a tail and the ground below.

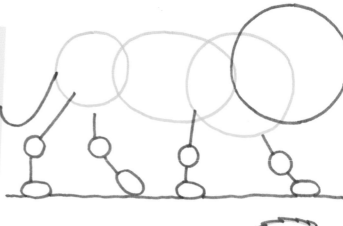

THE BIG ROAR!

Draw circles within circles. Eyes are shut if the mouth is wide open. Have fun adding teeth!

Step 3 ▶ Draw an outline around the legs and tail. Add a wedge for a head and small circles for a muzzle, then an eye and an ear. Draw a zigzag line for the neck and mane.

Step 4 ▶ Add pencil lines for the mane and shadows on the head, body and legs.

Step 5 ▶ Then colour in yellow, orange and brown, blending the colours carefully. Use several layers of one colour to get a darker shade.

Lion in action! (Scary!)

Step 1 ▶ Now for a different pose! Draw a big circle, an oval, and a smaller circle overlapping in a diagonal line.

Step 2 ▶ Add two circles for a head and mane. Draw lines and circles for legs, knees and paws.

Step 3 ◢ Draw in the head details. Look at the 'Roar' picture on the left to help. Add an outline around the body, legs and tail, with a zigzag mane.

Step 4 ▼ Colour in with creams or pale yellows. Now add a layer of dark yellow to the top half of the body. Use medium grey and brown for shadows and a soft pencil for shading and fur.

TOP TIP

Find pictures of different big cats to study and copy.

You can make a lion into a tiger by leaving off the mane and adding black and orange stripes. Or try a puma, leopard or panther!

7

Giraffe

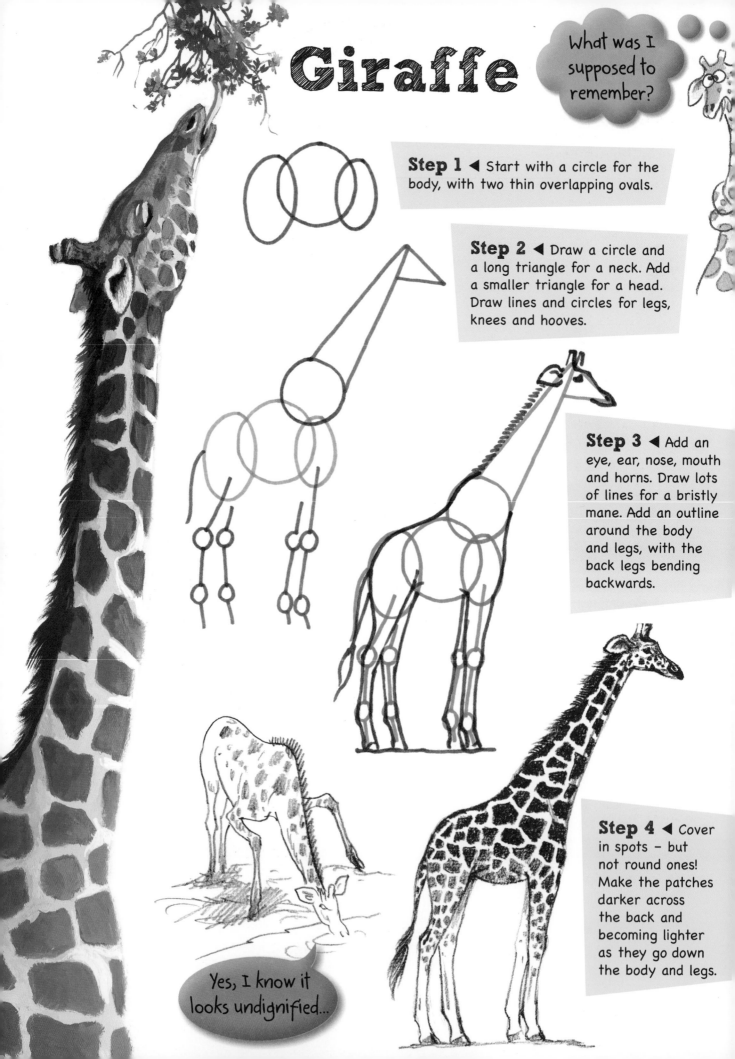

What was I supposed to remember?

Step 1 ◄ Start with a circle for the body, with two thin overlapping ovals.

Step 2 ◄ Draw a circle and a long triangle for a neck. Add a smaller triangle for a head. Draw lines and circles for legs, knees and hooves.

Step 3 ◄ Add an eye, ear, nose, mouth and horns. Draw lots of lines for a bristly mane. Add an outline around the body and legs, with the back legs bending backwards.

Step 4 ◄ Cover in spots – but not round ones! Make the patches darker across the back and becoming lighter as they go down the body and legs.

Yes, I know it looks undignified...

Mother and baby

Step 1 ▶ This time, draw the circles and ovals facing the other way. Add lines and circles for the legs, knees and hooves in midstride. Draw triangles and circles for the heads, necks and shoulders.

Step 2 ◀ Add the eyes, ears, noses, mouths and horns. Add lines for the mane and an outline around the body, thin legs and hooves.

Step 3 ▶ Colour in cream or pale brown, with darker brown across the backs. Shade between the legs and on the necks. Add bright orange and brown for spots. Use layers to make the patches on the backs darker.

Up a bit, Dad!

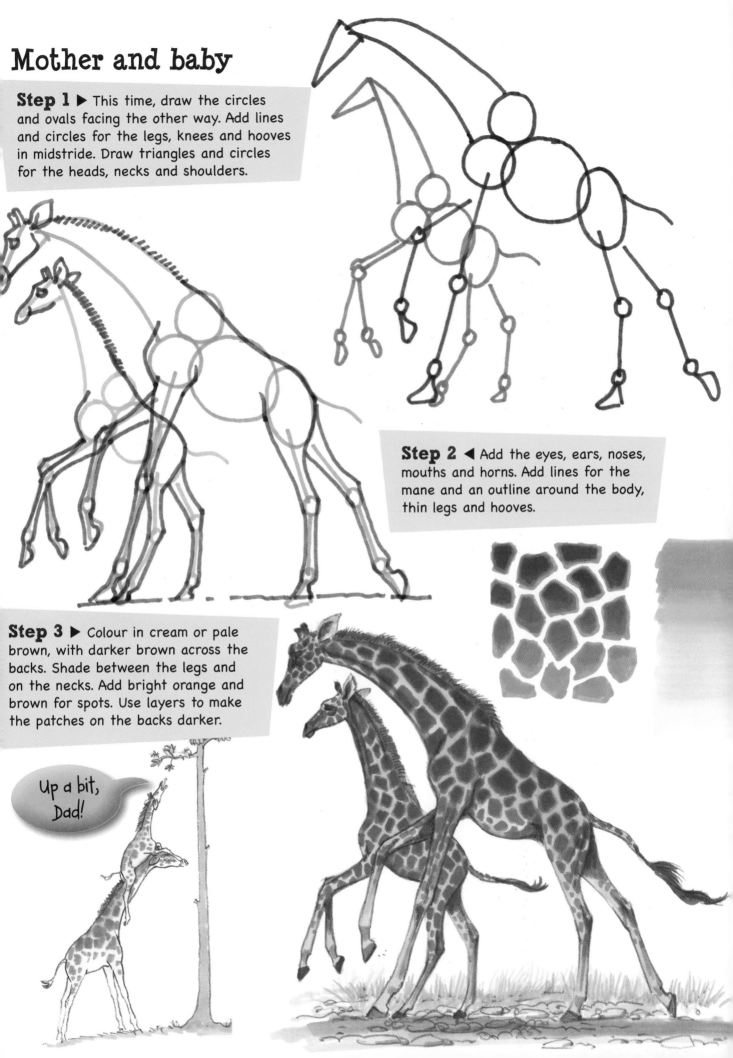

Rhino

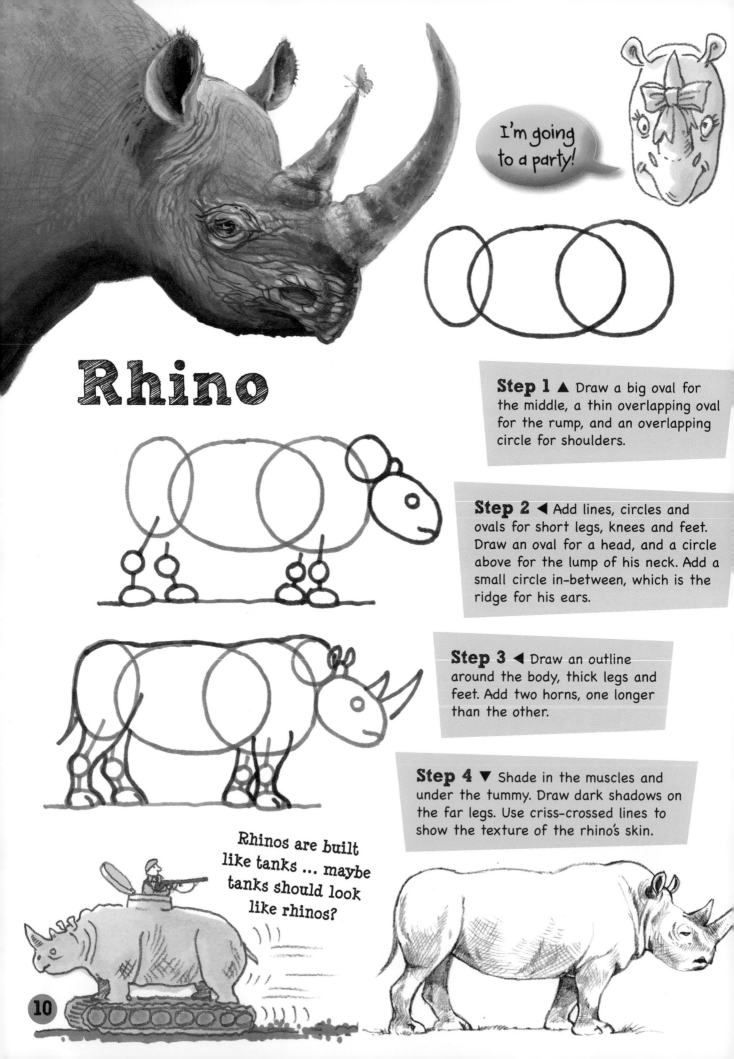

I'm going to a party!

Step 1 ▲ Draw a big oval for the middle, a thin overlapping oval for the rump, and an overlapping circle for shoulders.

Step 2 ◄ Add lines, circles and ovals for short legs, knees and feet. Draw an oval for a head, and a circle above for the lump of his neck. Add a small circle in-between, which is the ridge for his ears.

Step 3 ◄ Draw an outline around the body, thick legs and feet. Add two horns, one longer than the other.

Step 4 ▼ Shade in the muscles and under the tummy. Draw dark shadows on the far legs. Use criss-crossed lines to show the texture of the rhino's skin.

Rhinos are built like tanks ... maybe tanks should look like rhinos?

About to charge!

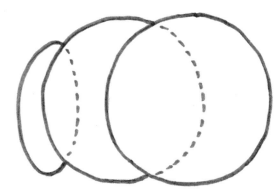

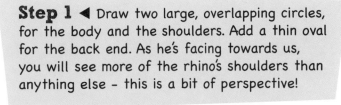

Step 1 ◀ Draw two large, overlapping circles, for the body and the shoulders. Add a thin oval for the back end. As he's facing towards us, you will see more of the rhino's shoulders than anything else – this is a bit of perspective!

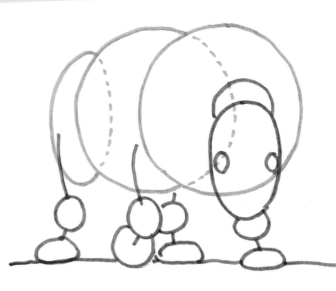

Step 2 ▶ Add an oval for a head, a half oval for a neck, and circles for the bony bits around his eyes. Draw lines and ovals for legs, knees and feet. Don't draw the legs too close together – rhinos are very wide!

Step 3 ◀ Draw his mouth, nostrils, horns and ears. Add an outline around the body and sturdy legs. Don't forget the huge oval toenails!

Step 4 ▶ Colour in shades of brown or grey, adding pink for the open mouth. Leaving a highlight along the back, draw in dark dramatic shadows on the near side and on the ground.

Oops!

LAST TREE IN THE DESERT

11

Wolf

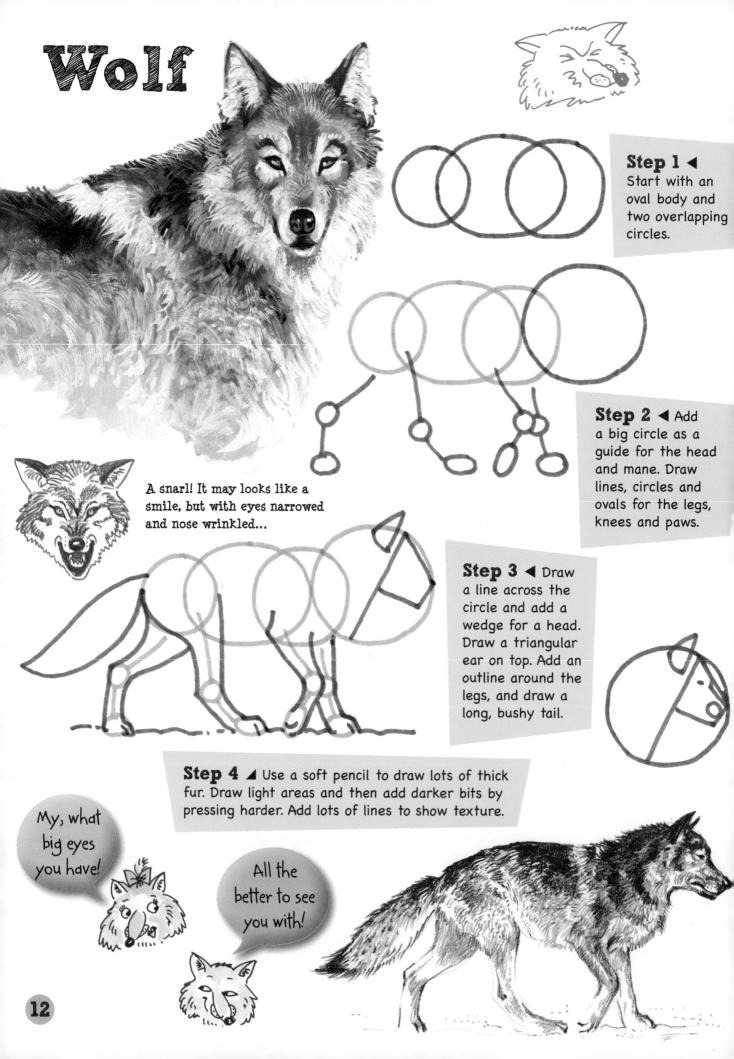

Step 1 ◀ Start with an oval body and two overlapping circles.

Step 2 ◀ Add a big circle as a guide for the head and mane. Draw lines, circles and ovals for the legs, knees and paws.

A snarl! It may looks like a smile, but with eyes narrowed and nose wrinkled...

Step 3 ◀ Draw a line across the circle and add a wedge for a head. Draw a triangular ear on top. Add an outline around the legs, and draw a long, bushy tail.

Step 4 ◢ Use a soft pencil to draw lots of thick fur. Draw light areas and then add darker bits by pressing harder. Add lots of lines to show texture.

My, what big eyes you have!

All the better to see you with!

Howling wolf

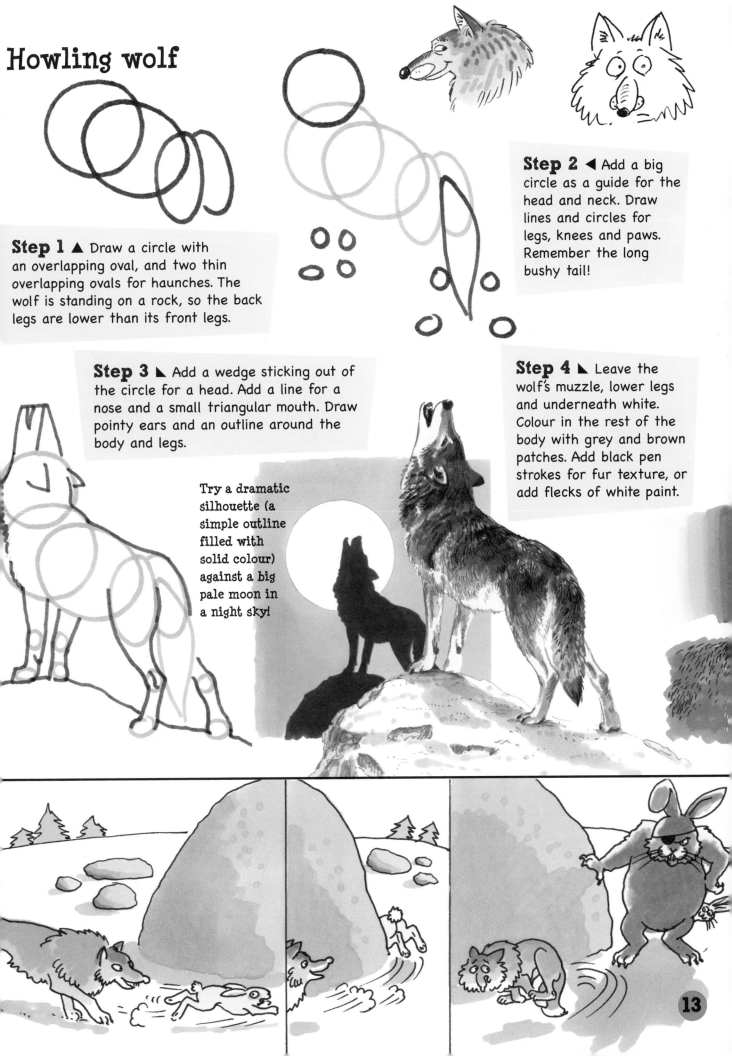

Step 1 ▲ Draw a circle with an overlapping oval, and two thin overlapping ovals for haunches. The wolf is standing on a rock, so the back legs are lower than its front legs.

Step 2 ◄ Add a big circle as a guide for the head and neck. Draw lines and circles for legs, knees and paws. Remember the long bushy tail!

Step 3 ◣ Add a wedge sticking out of the circle for a head. Add a line for a nose and a small triangular mouth. Draw pointy ears and an outline around the body and legs.

Try a dramatic silhouette (a simple outline filled with solid colour) against a big pale moon in a night sky!

Step 4 ◣ Leave the wolf's muzzle, lower legs and underneath white. Colour in the rest of the body with grey and brown patches. Add black pen strokes for fur texture, or add flecks of white paint.

13

Zebra

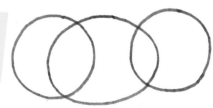

Step 1 ▶ Start simply again – an oval with two circles for the body.

Step 2 ▶ Add a triangle for a neck and a wedge for a head. Add a circle for a muzzle and line for a tail. Draw circles and lines for knees and walking legs. Remember, front legs and back legs bend differently!

Step 3 ▶ Draw a mouth, nose, cheek, ears and tail. Add an outline around the body, legs and hooves.

Step 4 ▼ Add stripes to your zebra. The stripes can be any shape as long as they are mostly vertical. Some zebras have black legs too!

How many zebras are in this herd? You can imagine a hungry lion getting sore eyes!

Two zebras fighting!

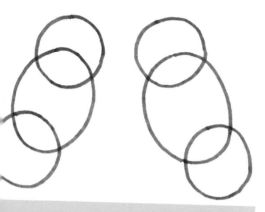

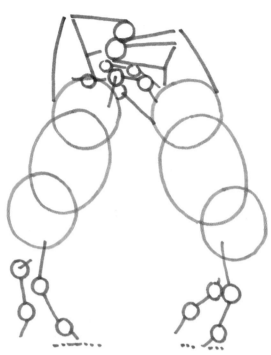

Step 1 ▲ Start by drawing ovals and circles at an upwards angle for the bodies. Leave room between them for the front legs.

Step 2 ▶ Add triangles for the necks and wedges for the heads. Draw circles for the muzzles. Add lines and circles for the legs, knees and hooves. The zebras' front legs are tangled together and their hind legs are on the ground.

Step 3 ▲ Draw an outline around the bodies, legs, hooves and tails. Add eyes, nostrils and ears flattened against the heads. You could miss out the hooves if you want to show them in a cloud of dust!

Step 4 ▲ Colour with light brown and pink shading. Add dark shadows before drawing the stripes. Use a fine black pen to make sure the stripes are neat.

Should zebras always be black and white? Use your imagination and go mad with your favourite colours!

Wildebeest

You always have to be different!

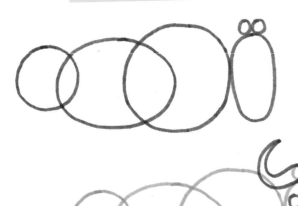

Step 1 ▼ Draw a small circle, an oval, and a big circle for the body. Add an oval for a head and two little circles on top.

Step 2 ▶ Add two small circles for eye sockets, an oval for a muzzle and nostrils inside. Draw lines and circles for legs, knees and hooves. Add a tail at the back and horns on the head – they look like a curly moustache!

Step 3 ◀ Draw an outline around the body, tail, legs and hooves. Add dots for eyes and curved lines for a long nose!

Step 4 ◀
Add dark stripes down from your wildebeest's shoulders. Draw a long, flowing mane. Add dark hair on the front of the face, but leave the rest light.

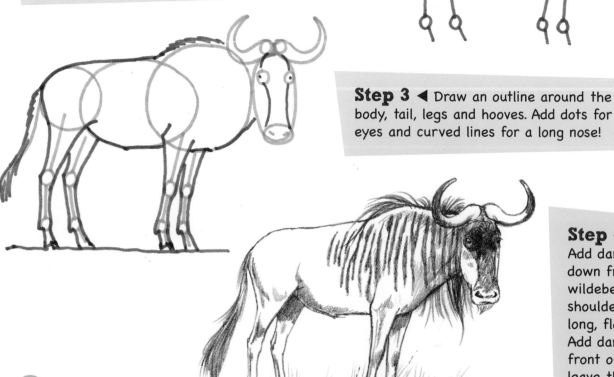

Wildebeest leaping

Step 1 ◣ This time, draw a big circle and add two ovals.

River ahead!

Mum?

Sorry!

It's cloudy today!

Hello?

My foot!

Ouch!

Who said that?

Step 2 ◣ Draw an oval for a head and add a muzzle, nostrils, eyes, and circles for horns. Add circles and lines for knees and stretched out legs. Draw a tail and a line along the back.

The African buffalo has curved horns like a moustache too!

Step 3 ◄ Draw an outline around the body, legs and hooves. Add lines for a mane and tail. Don't forget the nose and curly horns!

Step 4 ◄ Colour in pale grey all over. Add darker grey for shadows and pencil strokes for shading. Colour the mane and tail blue and add black shading over the top. See how the shading makes the horns look 3D!

Wildebeest are agile animals, and can jump. This one could be leaping up a hill, or jumping out of a river. You could even draw him trying to escape from the pouncing lion!

Come on, jump in!

17

Elephant

Step 1 ▼ Can it get any easier? Only two circles! Big ones though...

Step 2 ▶ Add two long, thin ovals for thighs. Draw lines, circles and ovals for legs, knees and feet. Add a small ear circle on the side of the head and a nose circle at the front.

Step 3 ◀ Draw an outline around the thick, solid legs and add toenails. Draw wedge-shaped ears from the ear circle on the head. Add a trunk from the nose circle and draw some tusks. Don't forget the eye and the wispy tail!

Step 4 ▶ Add lots of lines for creases and wrinkles, especially on the elephant's trunk and in between its legs. Draw the legs on the far side in shadow.

18

Rogue elephant charging!

Step 1 ▼ Start with the same two circles, but draw the smaller in front of the big one, like this.

Trunks are useful things!

trumpeting

sniffing

grasping

Step 2 ▲ Draw long ovals for thighs, circles for knees, and lines for legs. Add a nose circle and a raised trunk. Draw two half circles on the head.

sucking

squirting

Step 3 ◄ Draw big, flapping ears and tusks curving forwards. Draw an outline around the body, legs and tail. The back legs are thinner because they are further away. Don't worry about the feet – they're hidden in the dust!

Step 4 ▶ Colour in blue and grey, making the head, shoulders and legs at the front darker. This will make the back look further away. Add some pink to the tusks and wrinkle lines to the trunk. Use cross-hatched pencil lines to make the skin look leathery!

Eeek!

Boo!

Elephants can snorkel!

Details

Noses

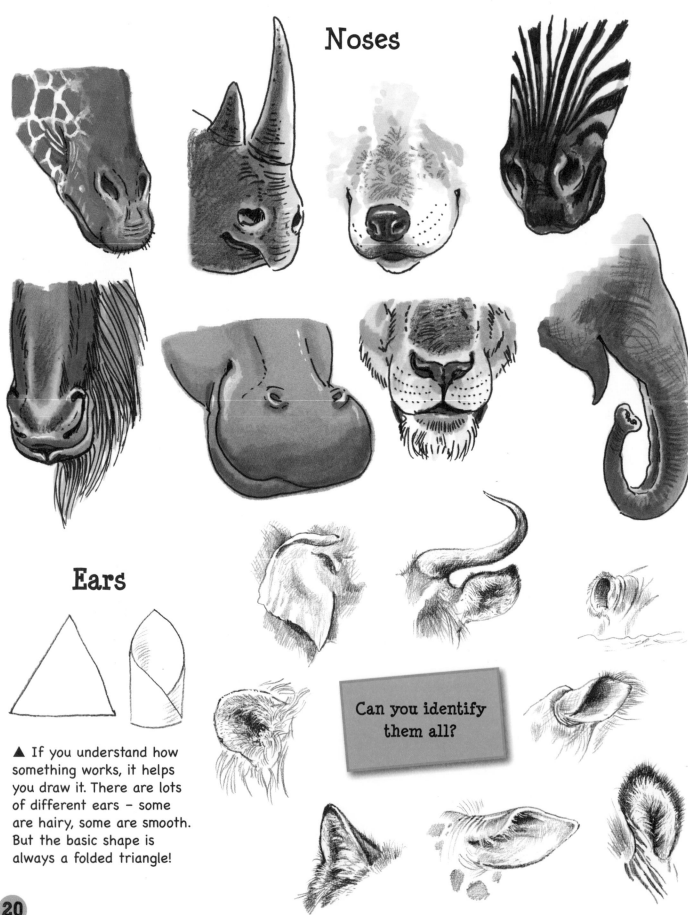

Ears

▲ If you understand how something works, it helps you draw it. There are lots of different ears – some are hairy, some are smooth. But the basic shape is always a folded triangle!

Can you identify them all?

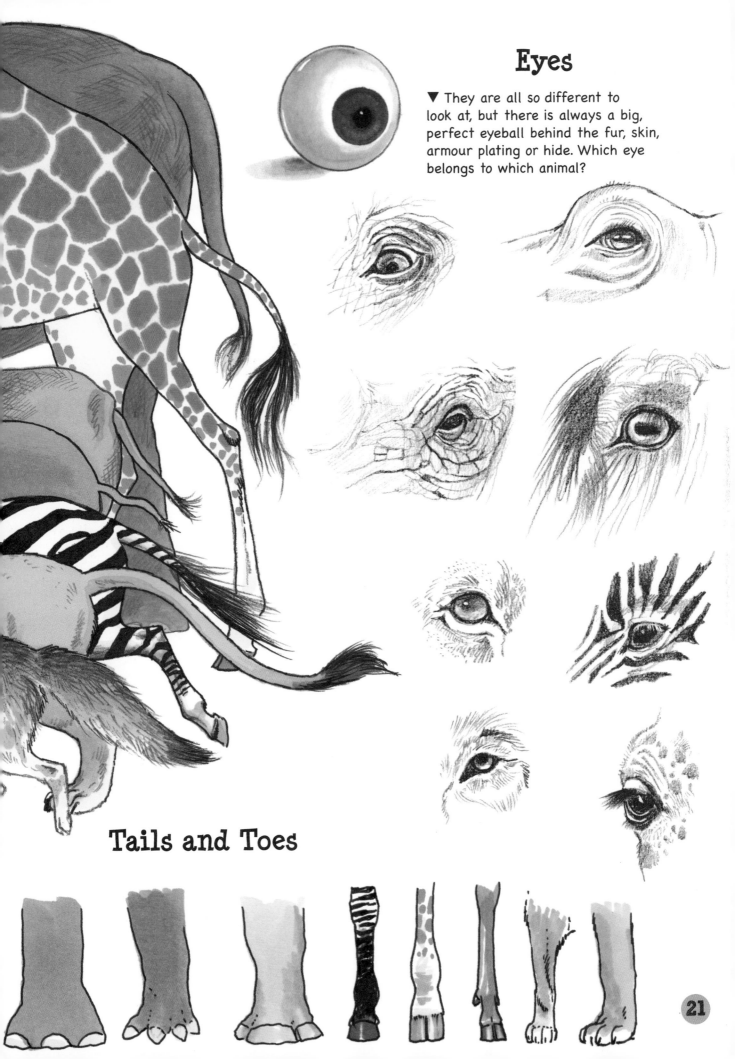

Eyes

▼ They are all so different to look at, but there is always a big, perfect eyeball behind the fur, skin, armour plating or hide. Which eye belongs to which animal?

Tails and Toes

Backgrounds

Simple is good!

Sometimes all you need is a few lines to show a spectacular landscape, such as a savannah...

...the African bush...

...or rocky terrain!

Hmph! Nothing for dinner here!

Want to show distance? Use pale and blue colours for things far away. Use stronger, brighter colours for things that are closer.

Cold landscape – use pale blues and greys, or leave the paper white for snow!

Brrrrr... It's cold!

Choose a background that is right for your animal!

Hot climate – use yellow and orange and strong contrasts.

Try a silhouette: draw an outline and fill it in carefully with black ink. Set it against a dramatic sky!

Phew... it's so hot!

Nice day!

I can't see anything...

Which way are we going?

Where are we?

Ouch! That was my toe!

Start SIMPLE

Practise your shapes – ovals,
circles, squares, wedges and
triangles.

Use goo
quality penc
double-end
pens. The
useful thick
ends which
great for
and b

Now let's put them together to create some great animal drawings!

Remember to use texture
and shading to make your
animals look realistic!

If your drawing doesn't look
quite the way you planned,
just have another go!

Don't forget, you can doodle just about anywhere, so long as you have some paper and a pencil!

Have fun!